THE HISTORY OF THE
MAYAN EMPIRE

HISTORY BOOKS FOR KIDS
CHILDREN'S HISTORY BOOKS

BABY PROFESSOR

EDUCATION KIDS

Speedy Publishing LLC

40 E. Main St. #1156

Newark, DE 19711

www.speedypublishing.com

Copyright 2017

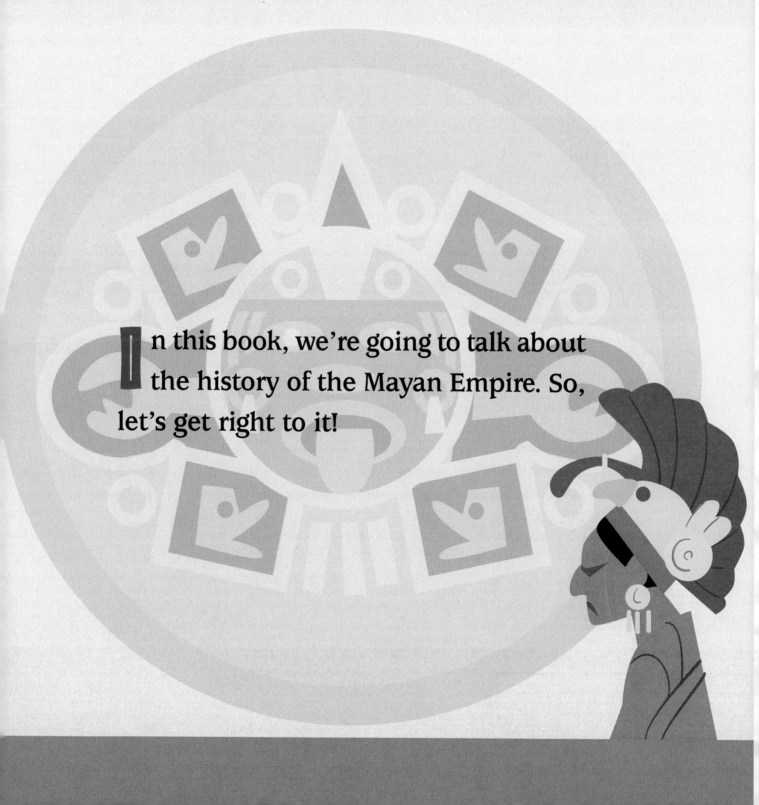

In this book, we're going to talk about the history of the Mayan Empire. So, let's get right to it!

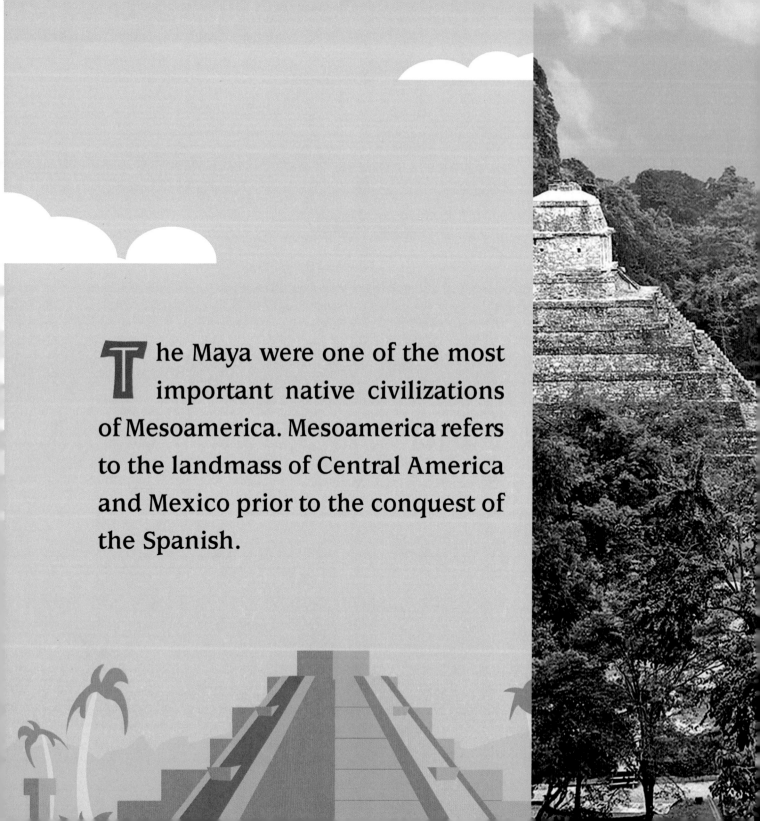

The Maya were one of the most important native civilizations of Mesoamerica. Mesoamerica refers to the landmass of Central America and Mexico prior to the conquest of the Spanish.

MAYAN EMPIRE RUINS

GUATEMALA CITY

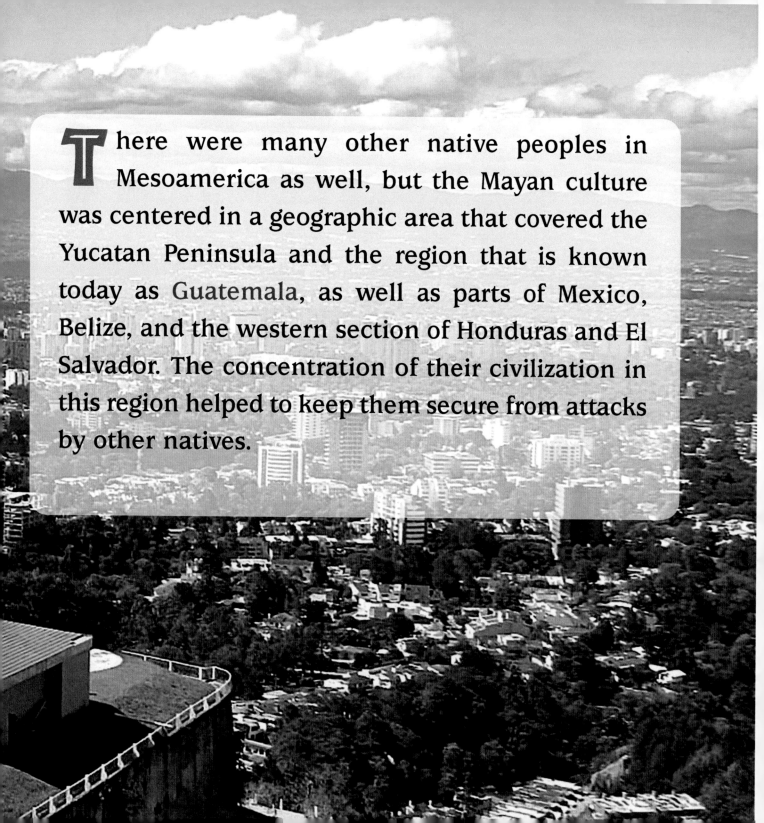

There were many other native peoples in Mesoamerica as well, but the Mayan culture was centered in a geographic area that covered the Yucatan Peninsula and the region that is known today as Guatemala, as well as parts of Mexico, Belize, and the western section of Honduras and El Salvador. The concentration of their civilization in this region helped to keep them secure from attacks by other natives.

MANY DIFFERENT LANGUAGES

The earliest Maya had one language, but by the Preclassic Period of their history, many different languages had evolved. Today, there are 5 million people living in the area where the Ancient Maya lived and they speak about 70 different Maya languages. Many of these people also speak Spanish.

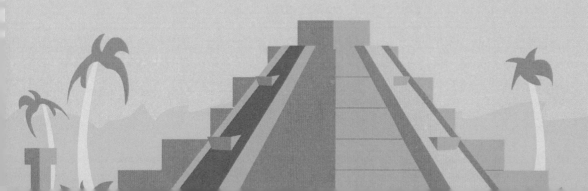

Within the large region of the Mayan culture, there were three different environmental areas. Eventually, the populations in these various groups had their own culture and language variances. These distinct populations lived in the following areas:

On the Yucatan Peninsula, specifically the northern lowlands

In the north section of Guatemala, in the Peten district, specifically its southern lowlands, and the nearby sections of Mexico as well as Belize and western Honduras

HAPPY VALLEY IN GUATEMALA

In the mountainous south section of Guatemala, in the southern highlands

From 250 AD to 900 AD, the Maya who lived in the southern lowlands built the enormous stone monuments and cities that have intrigued archaeologists since they were discovered.

THREE MAJOR TIME PERIODS

The Mayan Civilization has been divided into three major time periods as well as the time period when outside explorers made contact, which overlaps the Last Postclassic period.

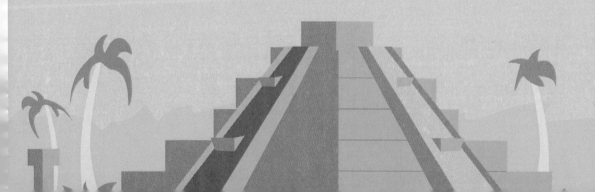

COBA

The Preclassic, Classic, and Postclassic periods have been divided as well:

- Preclassic from 2000 BC to 250 AD
- Early Preclassic from 2000 BC to 1000 BC
- Middle Preclassic from 1000 BC to 350 BC
- Late Preclassic from 350 BC to 250 AD
- Classic from 250 AD to 950 AD

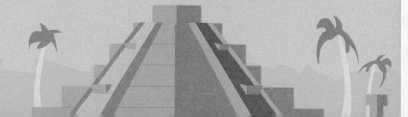

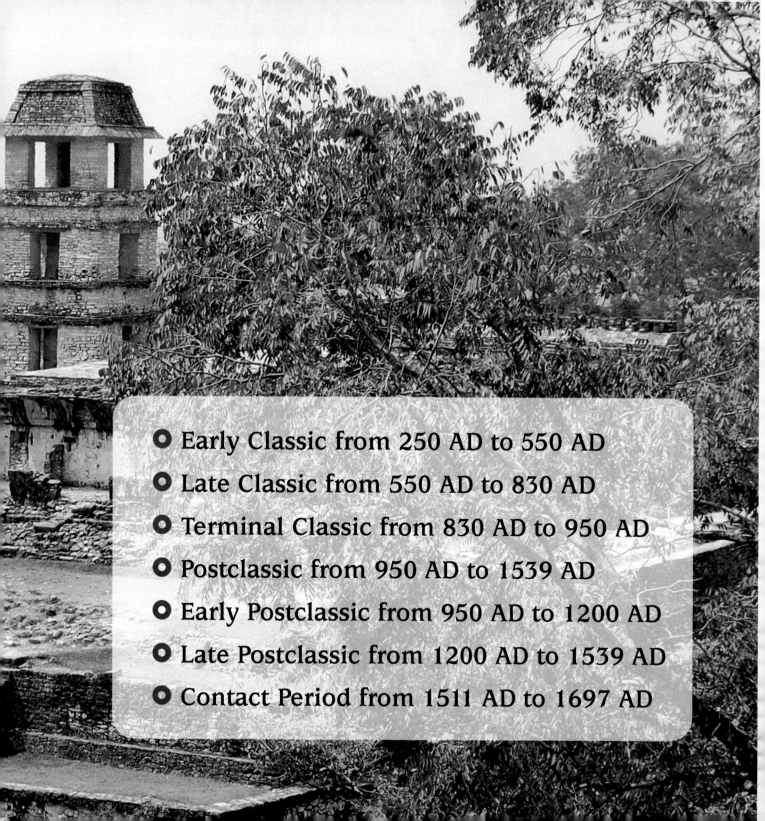

- Early Classic from 250 AD to 550 AD
- Late Classic from 550 AD to 830 AD
- Terminal Classic from 830 AD to 950 AD
- Postclassic from 950 AD to 1539 AD
- Early Postclassic from 950 AD to 1200 AD
- Late Postclassic from 1200 AD to 1539 AD
- Contact Period from 1511 AD to 1697 AD

CORN

THE PRECLASSIC PERIOD

The Preclassic Period of Mayan history was from 2000 BC to 250 AD. During this time, they grew crops and their society was based around agriculture. Corn was the most dominant crop, but beans, different varieties of squash, and cassava were grown as well. Mayan farmers began to spread out in the lowland and highland regions during the Middle Preclassic Period.

OLMEC COLOSSAL HEADS

The Middle Preclassic Period also gave rise to the Olmec civilization. This civilization had a huge influence on the Mayan as well as the Aztec civilizations.

MAYAN CALENDAR

The Maya adopted many of the Olmec religious practices and cultural traits. They also used the Olmec number system and their calendar.

In addition to their skills with agriculture, the Preclassic Maya had mastery of the building of pyramids, the planning and construction of cities, and the use of stone monuments for inscriptions.

TIKAL MAYAN RUINS

The great city of Mirador in the northern section of Peten was built during the Late Preclassic Period. Its size and complexity made the capital city of Tikal, which was built later

during the Classic Period, appear much smaller. The fact that the city of Mirador existed, proves that the Mayan civilization was thriving for centuries before its Classic Period.

MAYAN CITY OF PALENQUE

THE CLASSIC PERIOD

Beginning in 250 AD, the Mayan civilization reached its peak. During this golden age of their empire, the Maya constructed and populated about 40 cities including Tikal, Dos Pilas, Palenque, and Uaxactún. It's believed that the smallest cities had a population of 5,000 or more with the largest having upwards of 50,000 people. The civilization may have grown to 2 million or more in population.

The Maya had elaborate architecture and archaeologists have unearthed palace dwellings and temples for worship as well as large plazas and complex pyramid structures. They also had courts for ball games that were something like a combination of soccer and basketball. These ball games weren't just sports. They had religious and political significance. Those who lost the games were often offered up as sacrifices to the gods!

BALL COURT

The cities were built so they were surrounded by farms. Farmers used some advanced farming techniques, such as terracing as well as irrigation.

They also used "slash and burn," where an area of farmland is burned so the resulting ash makes the topsoil more fertile.

The Mayan gods were primarily associated with nature. The Maya worshipped gods of the sun, moon, and rain. They also had a god for the corn crops. The most important person in the Mayan society was the king, also called a holy lord.

MAYAN GOD CARVED IN THE ROCK

MAYAN KING ON THRONE SPEAKS TO A
WARRIOR IN FULL REGALIA

The people believed that the king was related to the deities. He acted as a mediator when communicating between the gods and the people. Part of the king's role was to perform the intricate rituals and religious ceremonies that were vital to their culture.

The Maya were accomplished artists and their temples were often built as pyramids with stepped surfaces. They decorated these structures with intricate reliefs and detailed inscriptions. Their religious rituals were connected with mathematics as well as astronomy. They understood the concept of "zero" in mathematics and they used a complicated calendar system based on the 365 days in a year.

The Mayan Calendar System and associated glyphs

names of days and associated glyphs

| Imix | Ik | Akbal | Kan | Chikchan | Kimi | Manik | Lamat | Muluk | Ok |
| Chuen | Eb | Ben | Ix | Men | Kib | Kaban | Etznab | Kawak | Ahau |

names of months and associated glyphs

| Pop | Uo | Zip | Zotz | Tzec | Xul | Yaxkin | Mol | Chen | Yax |
| Zac | Ceh | Mac | Kankin | Muan | Pax | Kayab | Cumku | Uayeb |

lords of the night and associated glyphs
(cycle of 9 days)

| G1 | G2 | G3 | G4 | G5 | G6 | G7 | G8 | G9 |

names of periods and associated glyphs

| Kin - 1 day | Uinal - 20 days | Tun - 360 days | Katun - 7200 days | Baktun - 144000 days |

At the beginning, modern scholars thought that the Maya were a peaceful civilization, but further research of their writings revealed that they were fierce warriors and that they fought bloody battles between their city-states. They also engaged in human torture and sacrifice as part of their worship practice.

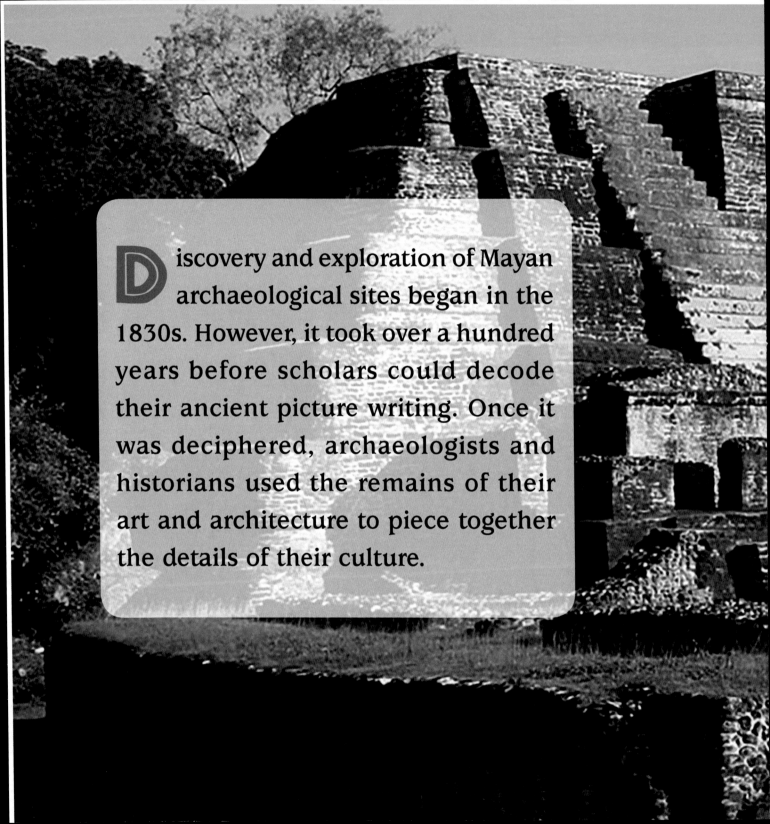

Discovery and exploration of Mayan archaeological sites began in the 1830s. However, it took over a hundred years before scholars could decode their ancient picture writing. Once it was deciphered, archaeologists and historians used the remains of their art and architecture to piece together the details of their culture.

ALTUN HA BELIZE

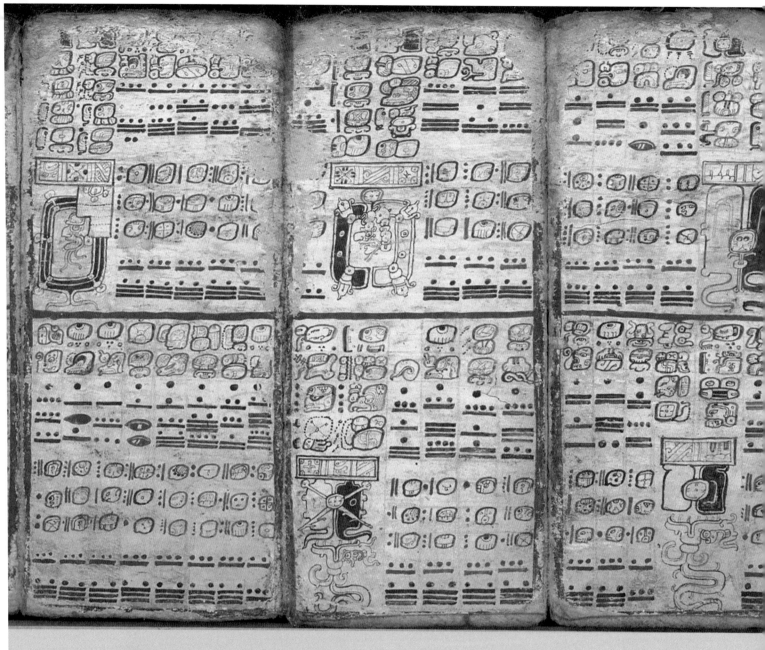

nscriptions on their monuments and buildings provided many details. The Maya also used tree bark for paper and created books.

F our of these books, called codices, have survived throughout the centuries for scholars to study.

RAINFOREST LIFE

Most native populations in Mesoamerica selected dry areas in which to live and then used available rivers to create irrigation systems to transport water for farming. However, in the southern lowlands there weren't many rivers for trade or transport.

MAYAN TEMPLES IN THE JUNGLE

At the beginning, scientists believed that the area where the Maya lived was a dense almost uninhabitable rainforest, but by the end of the 20th century it was determined that the climate there was more diverse.

In any case, the Maya made full use of the natural resources. They used available limestone for their building construction. They used obsidian, a rock formed from volcanic lava, to construct their tools and military weapons. They used salt for their food and jade for their decorative jewelry. Quetzal feathers were used to adorn the costumes of the Mayan leaders and shells were used to create trumpets for rituals and to sound the call to war.

THE MYSTERIOUS END OF THE MAYAN CULTURE

From 800 to 900 AD, the marvelous cities that the Maya had built in the southern lowlands were abandoned one by one. No one knows exactly what caused the end of this complex civilization although there are many theories.

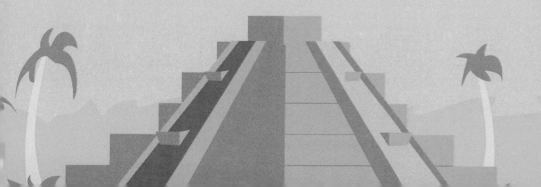

ome scholars think that the Maya had used up most of the resources surrounding their main cities and they no longer had enough to maintain the large population they had. Some historians think that the major cause was the never-ending bloody battles between the city-states and the political breakdown of the power of the kings and their dynasties.

TEMPLO DE LOS GUERREROS

TAJIN

They believe that because the people no longer revered their kings, the complex religious ceremonies that they had followed for centuries broke down causing a collapse of their culture. Yet another theory is that an enormous environmental change, such as a long period of intense drought, may have wiped them out. If this had occurred, it could have spelled immediate disaster since many of the large cities were dependent on rainwater both for drinking and for crops.

These three reasons, overpopulation and misuse of resources, political upheaval and warfare, as well as environmental disasters, such as droughts, may have all played a role in the end of this incredible ancient culture.

In the Yucatan highlands, a few cities, such as Chichén Itzá and Mayapán, continued to thrive during the Postclassic Period, but by the time the invaders from Spain set foot there in the 1500s, most of the stone cities had been completely covered over by rainforest vegetation.

Awesome! Now you know more about the history of the Mayan Empire. You can find more History books from Baby Professor by searching the website of your favorite book retailer.

Visit

BABY PROFESSOR
EDUCATION KIDS

www.BabyProfessorBooks.com

to download Free Baby Professor eBooks
and view our catalog of new and exciting
Children's Books

Made in the USA
Las Vegas, NV
26 July 2024